"BADASS POSITIVE AFFIRMATIONS FOR NEW PARENTS"

ALEX HOLMES

TABLE OF CONTENTS

Introduction 5

WHAT ARE AFFIRMATIONS? 13

The Value of Affirmations 19

How to Get the Most Out of This Book 21

Affirmations for *When You're Feeling Overwhelmed* 25

Affirmations for *Sleepless Nights* 35

Affirmations for *When You're Doubting Yourself* 39

Affirmations for *Your Emotional Validation* 45

Affirmations for *Parenting When You Feel Judged* 51

Affirmations for *When You Miss Your Pre-Baby Self* 57

Affirmations for *Successful Co-Parenting* 59

Affirmations for *When You Feel Worried* 61

Affirmations for *When You're Trying to Do It All* 65

Affirmations to *Empower You as a Parent* 71

Affirmations for *When It's Hard To Pack Up A Drawer* 77

Affirmations to *Reaffirm Your Individuality* 83

Finding Your Inner Voice 89

Implementing Affirmations in Your Life 91

Introduction

Oh, parenthood. There has never been anything more paradoxical and fuller of contradictions. Many parents would describe parenthood as both exhausting as well as purpose-giving. Being a parent is one of the most fulfilling experiences of a person's life. Among all the feelings humans can have, the joy of parenting is often one of the most profound. You'll never feel less like yourself while simultaneously feeling completely whole. Parenthood is a shocking life change, no matter how prepared you think you are. While becoming a new parent can be an extremely joyous and rewarding experience, it can also be a challenging and tumultuous time.

Many changes are made to a person's life when they become a parent, such as activities, sleep, health, roles, work, finances, and more. No wonder so many new parents feel like they're losing their minds in early parenthood, because, in a way, they are. They're losing their minds *as they know it*, and a new mind is being created from the ground up, due to this life-changing experience. Though becoming a parent is a beautiful and exciting time, the adjustment to this major change will be stressful and difficult for most new parents, and that is to be expected. Going into this new adventure with realistic expectations, as well as practical and mental health preparation, is vital for success and fulfillment.

There's such a weighty sense of responsibility you assume when you become a parent. Not only do you have to worry about all of the basic necessities like providing food, water, shelter, safety, and education, but it's also on you to provide a peaceful and enjoyable childhood, full of memorable moments for them to treasure. This can get so overwhelming, being the "magic maker" of their childhood, even though it's also a ton of fun. (Just another contradiction of parenthood...overwhelming, yet also fun.)

"Parent" is one of the most badass titles you can hold. However, it's hard to feel like a badass when you're sleep-deprived and covered in spit-up. I don't know about you, but when I was sleeping in two-hour spurts at a time, showering entirely too infrequently, and learning how to do this "mom" thing, I felt anything *but* badass. I felt lost, isolated, insecure, and overwhelmed. What I didn't realize at the time, though, is that these moments were building my badassery and empowering me over time. These moments are the kind of moments that develop you and create your strength.

Sometimes parenthood is just challenging. The truth is that no matter how positive, happy, and upbeat you are, no matter how put together you are, and no matter how many cutesy, perfect pictures you take, some days it's just really frustrating.

And guess what? It's okay.

Please know that you are not alone.

In this digital age, curated imperfection is running rampant. People are often cultivating an image or attitude of "imperfect perfection." They claim that they're being real and honest when, in fact, it's very surface-level "realness" in order to appear transparent.

It's a polished vulnerability filled with half-truths. While the community-building intentions behind this are good, parents *actually* need raw honesty and community, not vulnerability theater.

One of the biggest struggles I've found is getting to the point where I feel comfortable being honest and vulnerable about how hard it truly is. As parents, we don't want to express our opinions about the difficulty of parenthood, because we don't want to appear ungrateful. However, it's okay to just say that it's hard without wearing rose-colored glasses. Of course, you love your child. You don't need to clarify that to be able to vent about the difficulty of parenthood. The hard can just be hard without needing a silver lining. You're a parent, yes, but you're still a person too, and honesty comes with navigating the highs and lows of life.

Admitting that parenthood is challenging isn't a sign of unappreciation. A grateful heart is not dependent on loving things all the time. Gratitude is possible in the midst of challenge and difficulty. The emotions relating to parenthood are quite nuanced and sometimes complex. You can feel more than one emotion at a time, and you likely will in most scenarios of parenthood.

The unconditional love you feel for your child serves as fuel to get you through these long days of adjustment, information overload, and physical exhaustion. That powerful love is enough to make these days worthwhile, but it doesn't take away any of the complexity, confusion, and feelings of isolation or self-doubt. In order to combat any negative aspects of these new parenting days, we must refine the tools in our mental health toolbox.

Parental mental health is one of the most crucial and fundamental pieces of parenthood. Strong, positive mental health is often mistaken for simply "being happy." However, it's much deeper than just happiness. It comes from a place of true peace. You can't get to that place without intentionality. Regular affirmations are one of the most intentional things you can do for your mental health.

Affirmations rewire your brain. They are a very effective way to uplift and stabilize your mental health. Once you get into the habit of speaking affirmations to yourself, you'll likely begin speaking them over your children as well, teaching them how to empower themselves in this intentional way. Showing your children how to use affirmations to improve mental health is one of the best things you can do for them. They will learn how to do it by watching you.

When my children look up at me with full trust and genuine affection, when I know that I'm their safe place, those are the times when I feel like the ultimate badass. I put in the intentional hard work to accomplish this secure bond. I've worked so hard to create and foster an environment where my child feels safe, secure, and happy, despite what personal struggles I have navigated, and that's a strong thing to do. This inner strength I've found through parenthood has empowered me to begin to *believe* my own badassery. It hasn't happened overnight, as it is a process, but it's been a refining experience.

Mental health used to be a taboo topic, but our culture is seeing the positive shift that transparency around mental health provides. Positive mental health is crucial, especially in the early, new parenting days. It's always a productive idea to take preventative measures for your mental health however you can. Reaching out for help is necessary. It's not a sign of weakness; it's a sign of strength, resilience, and perseverance.

Sometimes, help may look like intervention, such as medication or therapy; help may also be as simple as implementing new, constructive daily routines. Among one of the simplest yet most impactful daily mental health routines are affirmations. Adding affirmations into your daily routine can be a game-changer. The simple act of saying affirmations each day can have a huge impact on your mental health and your life as a whole.

WHAT ARE AFFIRMATIONS?

Before we start implementing affirmations into our routines, we've got to know what they are and what their purpose is. Since parents rarely have enough free time, we definitely won't waste any of our limited time learning something without understanding *why* it's so helpful and necessary. Understanding the why is crucial to the effectiveness of the practice.

Affirmations are positive declarations that combat a negative mindset or destructive thought patterns. By utilizing affirmations, you can challenge and overcome self-sabotaging and negative thoughts. A daily affirmations routine is a helpful exercise for getting you into a constructive and positive mindset, strengthening your overall mental health. Parents need to have strong, stable, and positive mental health in order to be the best parent possible for their children. In short: you take care of yourself, and your children will ultimately benefit as a result of your stable and positive mental health.

Affirmations are a great tool for parents to utilize. They can help you get back on track when you're in a negative headspace. They can create a positive basis for your everyday mental health. Affirmations are short statements that work best if repeated throughout the day as needed. You can also repeat them in your head or aloud during an overwhelming or challenging parenting moment. A powerful way to recite affirmations is by saying them aloud as you look at yourself in the mirror. It may feel awkward at first to recite them aloud to yourself in the mirror, but each time you do it, it'll feel a little more comfortable. The impact of this is so compelling.

It might be difficult to remember helpful affirmations in the heat of the moment, so you may find it beneficial to post little note cards with written affirmations on them throughout your bedroom or home. My favorite way to quickly display affirmations is by writing them on my mirror with a dry-erase marker. (Pro tip: A dry-erase marker on a bathroom mirror works better than a wet-erase marker because the condensation from the shower in the bathroom will cause the wet-erase writing to smear and even completely ruin it.)

Answer the questions below with the utmost honesty. No one will know your answers unless you want them to. Tap into your deepest vulnerability and don't hold back. This intentional self-improvement work can be difficult, but the results of it are overwhelmingly profound. You deserve the best, and you play the most vital role in accomplishing the best for yourself.

What do you struggle with the most?

_____

_____

_____

How would your life change if you were able to reform your mental health in the area mentioned above?

_____

_____

_____

What are your favorite aspects of parenthood?

_____

_____

_____

What has surprised you about parenthood?

_____

_____

_____

Visualize your ideal perfect day or moment of true peace. What does it consist of?

_____

_____

_____

How can you implement more of these peaceful aspects in your daily life?

_____

_____

_____

What are your long-term mental health goals?

_____

_____

_____

Let's work on achieving this together!

The Value of Affirmations

Why are affirmations important?

Affirmations help you to learn, solidify, and ultimately believe your value. Declaring positive affirmations over yourself and your parenting is essential for keeping an uplifting and healthy mindset. The power of positive thinking should not be undervalued. Positive affirmations can help you flip the script. If you're thinking or speaking negatively about yourself, affirmations will assist you in combating it and flipping the negative direction back to a positive one.

Affirmations convince you, over time, that you are enough.

You can do this.

Repetition is important with affirmations. For best results, be sure to repeat them at least twice a day and throughout each day as needed. Sometimes, you may have to make it up as you go along. "Fake it til you make it" as they say.

There is so much power in speaking truth over yourself even when you don't believe it. If you say it enough, you'll eventually believe it! Even if you don't feel the sentiments that your repeated affirmation is stating, your perseverance and diligence in saying it regularly, regardless of if you believe it or not, will pay off. You might not ever fully believe your affirmation, but with time, you will at least begin to feel a sense of empowerment as a result of saying it.

How to Get the Most Out of This Book

The most useful way to use this book is in whatever way works best in your personal daily life routines. The point of this book is to provide you with helpful and encouraging insights that you can practically apply to your life, in hopes that over time these affirmations will help empower you as a parent. If you're not able to apply them to your life regularly, they won't be as effective. Whatever method or strategy works best for you in your current season of life, ensuring regular use of these affirmations, is the best strategy for getting the most out of this book!

I've read so many great self-help books that have awesome insight and useful tools, but a lot of the specific methods recommended don't work or adapt well in my current season of life. What ends up happening is that I try to adapt to them, fail to do so due to circumstantial reasons, and then feel defeated even more than I did to begin with.

I realized over time that, for me to implement new routines and helpful strategies in my mental health routines, I have to choose whatever route is most realistic for what my days are looking like in my current circumstances. This can change from season to season! It's also not always linear. To put it simply, you can get the most out of this book by implementing it in your routines as realistically as possible. It doesn't have to be perfect to be effective. There's no one perfect, correct way to do it.

This book is meant for you to take what you need when you need it. Instead of a traditional chapter format, this book functions more like a glossary of affirmations that target specific scenarios and emotions. That way, whenever you need perspective and encouragement in specific situations, you know exactly how and where to effectively find what you need.

There are some guided questions throughout the book to provoke deeper exploration within yourself as desired. Sometimes, for me, this looks like flipping through to the section I need while hiding in my bedroom closet to create a singular moment of peace, repeating my affirmation, and getting back out there to those little humans. The bottom line: Take what you need from this book and move on with your day feeling more confident.

It is my sincere hope that you are comforted and empowered by the sentiments in this book.

Affirmations for
When You're Feeling Overwhelmed

―――――――――――――
•●•

"THIS IS TEMPORARY."

S ometimes, you just need to realize the power of "someday." Someday, you'll fit back in those jeans. Someday, you won't be needed as much. Someday, you won't have multiple little hands touching all over you. Someday, you won't be soothing a fussy baby all hours of the night. Realizing that these all-consuming moments are fleeting can help you put things in perspective more efficiently. These hard moments in the trenches of parenthood are temporary and won't last forever. I say that not to invalidate how you're feeling now; your feelings are completely valid. Sometimes, it can feel frustrating hearing the "you're going to miss this" sentiments while you're trudging through the thick of hard parenting seasons. However, I just mean to offer a zoomed-out perspective.

It can be hard to realize the hard moments are temporary because they feel never-ending. In the early newborn days with my first child, I remember crying to my husband about how I felt like I'd never do anything outside of care tasks ever again. Now that my kids are older, I see there's so much more that I do, but at the time, it felt like all I was good for was changing diapers, pumping breast milk, and staying up all night.

Another perspective to consider is that, someday, your house will be quiet. Someday, there won't be tiny laundry items to fold. Someday, you will get to drink your coffee while it's hot. In life, there are seasons. Some seasons are more all-consuming than others, but each season has its own little mercies.

"I'M DOING THE BEST I CAN."

This is probably my most-used affirmation. I find myself repeating this one in my head over and over throughout the day, as it's such a valuable reminder. Somedays, your best will look like a perfectly tuned schedule and a day full of beautiful moments. On other days, you'll be barely hanging on. No matter the context or circumstances, your best **is** good enough. Not every season of life will be a winning season. Some seasons are just pure survival, especially the newborn phase.

Even when you're just doing the bare minimum, that is enough.

Believe it or not, you are the perfect parent for your children. You have been given these specific children for a reason. You were made for one another. As humans, we are hardwired to innately desire strong, positive bonds with our parents. Even on the bad days, they still think the world of you.

We are our own worst critics. Too often, we get wrapped up in the unrealistic expectations of perfectionism in our culture. Relinquishing the hold of perfectionism over your parenting will bring you freedom. This affirmation is a step forward in that process.

"I AM NOT DEFINED BY ONE BAD DAY."

Okay, we all have bad days. That's no secret. However, what is most important is how we deal with our bad days. I can't tell you how many times I've uttered the phrase, "I just feel like such a bad mom." But really, what is a bad mom or a bad parent? I would venture to guess that this definition varies depending on whom you ask.

Throughout our lives, we *will* fail our children. They will fail us, too. It's inevitable. Sometimes, we may fail them in a way only they perceive, such as not letting them sleep over at a friend's house or not letting them have a cookie when they want to. Other times, we may truly fail them. We may be too impatient, unfairly unloading our emotions. We may make mistakes and truly wrong them. However, what would make a "bad parent" is one who sees their wrongdoings yet refuses to acknowledge or fix them. A parent who recognizes their shortcomings and actively works to fix them is the best type of parent around.

As the parent, you set the tone of the emotional environment of your household. Children are extremely perceptive (yes, even infants) and they can pick up on and internalize the energy we're putting out there. It's important to remember that our children are human, too. They deserve respect, even though we're in a position of authority over them. Never be too proud to apologize to your children, even when they're too young to understand.

Starting this mutually respectful environment begins at birth. When you apologize to your child, don't simply leave it at that. Take it a step further and humbly ask for their forgiveness. This teaches them the importance of showing respect to others and strengthens your bond with them. Even though your infant may not fully understand, they will be able to grasp the environment over time, resulting in a respectful and collaborative home.

There is immense power in the intentionality of saying, "I forgive you," instead of, "It's okay." When a person hears "I forgive you," they can begin forgiving themselves and moving forward. Cultivating this environment begins in early parenthood days.

Parents and children are not adversarial enemies; we are a team. Each generation has worked hard to refine and improve the parent and child relationship, and over time, we have seen the benefits of nurturing a closer bond.

There is a phrase I used to say frequently when I taught preschool that has honestly given me so much solace as an adult. *"It's never too late to turn it around."* You are never too far gone to make adjustments.

Intentionality is key. Mistakes are inevitable. Forgiveness is healing.

"I WILL FORGIVE MYSELF."

Even when your child is a newborn, learning how to have forgiveness for yourself is so important. Listen to me when I say that you WILL make mistakes as a parent. Making mistakes is a part of life. You will inevitably make mistakes along your parenthood journey. Everyone makes them, even the most "perfect" and experienced parents.

The good news here is that mistakes present an opportunity to learn and grow. Every mistake offers a lesson for you to learn from. Once your lesson is learned, you've got to release the guilt. Guilt has no place in parenthood. We all want what is best for our children, so guilt is natural to feel. However, it is not helpful when it fuels feelings of inadequacy or causes you to render harsh judgments of yourself. Negative feelings towards yourself can spill over into your parenting, ultimately affecting your child.

Keeping realistic expectations for yourself is a crucial element of avoiding parental guilt. For your standards to be realistic, they should come from your best judgment and be tailored to your needs. Set your expectations for yourself based on your strengths and weaknesses, your responsibilities and circumstances, and the characteristics of your child.

Remember, there is not one "right" or perfect way to do things. Make sure you're not holding yourself to an unrealistic set of standards made up by someone else. You get to bring your own individualized method of parenting to the table, and that's part of the beauty of it.

"I WILL CHOOSE TO FOCUS ON GRATITUDE."

Choosing gratitude or having "an attitude of gratitude" sounds like a cutesy little happy idea that you might see on a decorative sign at Target. However, it is not easy to do, especially in the trenches of early parenthood. It's difficult to feel grateful when you're clouded by sleep deprivation and unrealistic societal expectations of parents. Choosing gratitude isn't just something to think about and sometimes utilize; it's a way of living. Once you begin to implement gratitude routines in your life, you and your family will reap the rewards.

The key to gratitude is optimistic intention.

I'd often find myself lamenting: *"How can I choose gratitude when my basic needs aren't being met? How can I choose gratitude when there are so many things I want to change but can't yet?"* Choosing gratitude doesn't mean that everything is perfect. It simply means you're choosing to be grateful for what you *do* have, regardless of your circumstances. Focusing on the good and thinking about what you *do* have, instead of harping on what you don't have, helps refine this perspective of gratitude.

A practical way that you could cultivate gratitude within yourself, and your household, is a daily gratitude journal where you list 3 to 5 things each day that you're grateful for, no matter how small. You could also make gratitude a part of your daily routine together by facilitating a "gratitude scavenger hunt" either by yourself or with your children! While your kids are little, you will have to model this behavior for them, but as they mature, they will start to participate as well. Feel free to use the checklist below to assist in your gratitude scavenger hunt.

Gratitude
Scavenger Hunt

- ☐ FIND SOMETHING THAT MAKES YOU HAPPY
- ☐ FIND SOMETHING THAT MAKES YOU FEEL SAFE
- ☐ FIND SOMETHING THAT MAKES YOU LAUGH
- ☐ FIND SOMETHING THAT IS YOUR FAVORITE COLOR
- ☐ FIND SOMETHING THAT SMELLS GOOD
- ☐ FIND SOMETHING THAT SOUNDS BEAUTIFUL
- ☐ FIND SOMETHING THAT IS USEFUL TO YOU
- ☐ FIND SOMETHING THAT REMINDS YOU OF HOME
- ☐ FIND SOMEONE WHO YOU LOVE
- ☐ FIND SOMETHING THAT YOU ENJOY DOING

Affirmations for
Sleepless Nights

"I WILL SLEEP AGAIN. THIS IS TEMPORARY."

When you're in the trenches of early parenthood, it truly feels never-ending. You may be feeling like you'll never get a night of solid sleep again. The lack of sleep in new parenthood usually comes as a shock. Of course, you know going into parenthood that your child will need you in the nighttime, resulting in new sleep patterns for yourself. But *feeling* this prolonged physical exhaustion is another story. There's no way to prepare yourself for what an extended lack of sleep feels like and how it will impact your well-being.

"Sleep when the baby sleeps." Okay...So should I fold laundry when the baby folds laundry? We can't just let everyday responsibilities fall by the wayside simply because we have a newborn. Someone's gotta do it. "Sleep when the baby sleeps" is a well-intentioned phrase that is not helpful. I remember feeling so frustrated in the newborn days when people would tell me this phrase because the reality of my new workload was setting in and I was struggling to balance it all. As much as I would've loved to neglect all other responsibilities and just "sleep when the baby sleeps," this was not realistic for me, and I imagine the same is true for many parents.

Also, when someone tells an exhausted parent to just "sleep more," it's likely not going to end well. I always thought (and sometimes even retorted in response): "Yeah, I'd love to sleep more! Want to babysit my kid so I can?" People change their tune pretty quickly after that.

Self-compassion and encouragement are two things we all need more of. Trying to get adequate sleep for your child can be a lonely struggle when the world does not support parents or developmental sleep norms. Adequate sleep is vital for positive mental and physical health outcomes. It's difficult to think rationally when sleep is in short supply. Sometimes, you may need to "fake it til you make it," and reassure yourself that sleep will improve for you and your baby over time.

This is where the above affirmation comes in. Telling yourself over and over that this is indeed temporary, and you actually *will* sleep again may help shift your perspective and give you the encouragement you need to power through. In the meantime, as you wait for a season with extended, restful sleep, make sure to find coping strategies and a balanced routine with your partner or those in your parenting support circle.

"THE SLEEPING PATTERNS OF MY BABY ARE NOT A REFLECTION OF MY PARENTING."

Sleep regressions, frequent wakeups, nap strikes...All of these sleep issues are so frustrating, especially for an already sleep-deprived parent. It's even worse when you feel you've tried everything to help your child and solve these problems. It's important to remember that these sleep changes and issues are not your fault! Most sleep issues and changes are due to developmental growth or a change of schedule.

"AS A PARENT, I CANNOT CONTROL MY BABY'S SLEEP, BUT I CAN GIVE THEM LOVE AND SUPPORT TO NAVIGATE SLEEPING PATTERNS."

Sometimes, the best thing you can do for your child is just to simply be there. Sleep struggles can feel scary and frustrating to a baby. Babies are designed to need their parents. The warmth of a parent's love and touch is extremely comforting to a child. Remember, they're not doing this on purpose to frustrate you. They're not doing this *to* you; they just *need* you. This affirmation serves as a practical reminder to you that bumps in the road regarding your baby's sleep are not caused by you, and that you have a vital role in supporting them through it.

Affirmations for

When You're Doubting Yourself

There is no place for self-doubt in parenting. Unfortunately, it's inevitable. "Mom guilt" has become a notorious concept in our culture because it's so widely experienced. There are plenty of memes on the internet themed around mom guilt and parental guilt. Jokes about parents counting down to bedtime all day because they're so exhausted from parenting, but then once the kids go to bed, they spend most of their free time looking through photos of the kids and missing them. (Just another one of those fun paradoxical situations in parenthood.)

"I AM ENOUGH."

Having a strong foundation of self-worth is so important, not just in parenting, but in life as a whole, because of the security it provides. This inner security empowers our parenting. To cultivate a vibrant, fruitful life for us and our children, we have to believe in our worthiness. The ripple effect of believing you are enough is much more widespread than you probably think. We can positively influence those around us simply by embracing our self-worth.

It's possible to be enough as you are right this moment, while also working on improving yourself. Whether you evolve and change or stay just as you are, either way, you are enough.

Take a moment to say it out loud: "I am enough. Just as I am, right here, right now, I am enough." Observe how you feel as you say this. Other than likely feeling silly talking to yourself, is it difficult for you to say it?

_____

_____

_____

Why do you think that is?

_____

_____

_____

What can you do today to work towards a strong sense of self-worth?

_____

_____

_____

Think about who you are just as you are right now. What are some positive traits about you?

_____

_____

_____

Think about your ripple effect. What relationships in your life would be stronger or happier due to some empowerment within yourself?

_____

_____

_____

"I CAN DO THIS."

Sometimes, we just need to hear this. There is a special power in saying it yourself, to yourself.

I've never questioned my abilities more than I have in parenthood. Obstacles in life can cause us to doubt our strengths and abilities. Some choose to let failures and obstacles define them. They succumb to the disappointment and settle. Others use obstacles and failure as a motivator to move forward. The results we achieve will be determined by our internal faith in ourselves. Keep getting back up again.

"I TRUST MY PARENTAL INSTINCTS."

Every parent is given an innate discernment tool known as natural instinct. This is sometimes referred to as "a mother's intuition" or "mom gut," but this natural parenting instinct isn't just inherited or experienced by mothers. Fathers and all parents experience it as well.

Don't stress yourself out if you don't feel your parental instinct kick in right away. A parental instinct is developed and strengthened over time. If this instinct does not feel natural to you at first, that's okay! You will get there eventually. Be patient with yourself and extend yourself some grace.

"I BECOME A BETTER PARENT DAY AFTER DAY."

Children are like little sponges; they absorb everything they see and hear. You are always setting an example for your child whether you try to or not. Throughout your journey together, you will learn and grow alongside one another. They will watch you learn from mistakes and build resilience. You will be able to model positive growth for them simply by being you.

Parenting has no ultimate destination. No one is an immediate expert when they first begin participating in something. You cannot and will not know everything. But what you will do is constantly learn. You'll find your parenting style and preferences over time. With this constant growth and learning, you will become a better parent day by day.

Each day you'll learn a little more, and when you look back after a while, you'll be able to take note of all the wonderful knowledge, skills, and experiences you've acquired.

Be the person you want your child to grow up to be.

Affirmations for

Your Emotional Validation

"MY FEELINGS ARE VALID."

Being honest about your feelings and being brave enough to work through them, actually helps your children understand emotions better and works to develop their emotional intelligence over time. On a rainy October afternoon, during a particularly heated exchange with my four-year-old, we found ourselves amid an emotional breakthrough. I expressed to her my frustration with how the day was going and with the conflict we were experiencing, and she said something that stuck with me. "Parents can feel mad and frustrated too?" This led us to a conversation about honesty and emotions, and this conversation humanized me to her.

"MY FEELINGS DON'T DEFINE ME."

Emotions are indicators to communicate a need within our minds and bodies. Even though they can be chaotic and complex, they are there to guide you, not to control you. If you're feeling sad, that doesn't mean you are a sad or negative person inherently. It simply means you're sad. And it's okay to be sad. The emotions you feel are integral to who you are, but they do not constitute who you are.

"I DESERVE TO FEEL SEEN AND REGARDED."

Wanting to feel and be seen is an innate desire we all have to varying degrees. The isolation parenthood causes can make a person feel invisible. Lack of visibility in parenthood can lead to further mental health issues during the already-vulnerable time of early parenthood.

I see this innate desire of wanting to be seen with my daughter. Every night and every nap once I tuck her in, do our routine, and head out her bedroom door, we always do the "I love you" sign language sign to one another. She would always call me back into the room to say, "Do you see me?!" to make sure I saw her sign back to me. It was cute at first, but it quickly became frustrating because, honestly, I was too impatient and was ready to put her down to sleep. Eventually, it clicked to me: She just wants to be *seen*. She wants her love-the tangible representation of her love-to be acknowledged so that I would know her heart, and so she would feel visible.

We all have this desire within us. We just want to be seen and heard. You deserve for your emotions to be communicated just as much as the people around you. Don't sell yourself short.

"THE FEELINGS I HAVE ARE OKAY TO HAVE."

Parenthood is indeed amazing, refining, and purpose-giving. However, there are plenty of frustrating moments, days, and phases. It is okay not to love every moment. You are not a bad parent for sometimes resenting certain situations. You're not a bad parent if you don't love every single thing about parenthood. You're human, and you're allowed to be human and experience human emotions in addition to being a parent.

As long as your feelings aren't putting you or others in harm's way, you are absolutely justified in feeling what you feel. It's best to allow yourself to work through your complex emotions in order to accept them and move forward. As your child grows older, they will greatly benefit from watching you healthily and constructively process hard emotions.

"I DESERVE TO BE HAPPY."

One of the most sacrificial entities a person can engage in is parenthood. Once you become a parent, your child and their needs always come first. This can feel shocking in the beginning since, up until this point in life, you've only ever had to worry about satisfying your own needs.

It is common for new parents to continuously place the needs of others before their own, resulting in a reprioritization of individual needs. Just because it's common doesn't mean that it's the right thing to do. Taking care of ourselves is the only way we will be able to continue providing for those who depend on us constantly. The key to caring for your child while also enjoying parenthood is taking care of yourself, physically and mentally.

As you settle into parenthood, you'll quickly get used to putting your children's needs above yours. Over time, this will become second nature and, eventually, it may even result in unintentional neglect of your own needs. Of course, your child's needs must be prioritized, but not at the expense of your needs. Your needs have to be accommodated as well as theirs. Sometimes, you may lose sight of the fact that, yes, you also deserve to be happy, not just the people around you. It's a constant balancing act, but you deserve happiness just as much as the other people in your household and life.

List three things that make you feel the happiest.

Affirmations for

Parenting When You Feel Judged

• ● •

It's far too common for strangers to force themselves in and share their opinions about everything these days. Social media has made this so much worse. Judgmental Judy can sit behind her keyboard and freely speak her mind about another parent's choices, not knowing any context or knowing the people she's judging at all. There are pros to social media and a virtual sense of community, but the unsolicited judgment so easily given is not fun. Social media isn't the only place where the unsolicited judgment of parents occurs. All you need to do is step into your local grocery store with your child, and likely someone will have something to say.

"I WILL NOT ALLOW STRANGERS TO SHAME ME OR MY PARENTING CHOICES."

You can't control how other people act or what they say. However, you can control how you respond and to what level you allow it to bother you.

Judgment and shame are among some of the worst things to experience, especially as a parent. Parenting is hard enough as it is, and it just feels unfair when strangers and outsiders make it even more difficult by offering their unwelcome advice and opinions. It seems like everyone has an opinion these days, especially about children and parenthood. It's important to remember that, ultimately, the only opinions that should matter are yours and your partner's opinions.

"I DECIDE WHICH PARENTING ADVICE I UTILIZE."

It sounds simple but it's worth repeating: You don't have to listen to and internalize it all. You get to decide what parenting advice and opinions you take, and which ones you choose to disregard. You get to choose what parenting advice you ultimately internalize. Once you decide to not let others' opinions about your parenting choices affect your thinking, you will feel liberated. This will also help you walk in your own individuality as a parent.

I remember taking my oldest child when she was one month old to Home Goods on an early April day, already overwhelmed by even doing the outing in general. We needed a new rug, and I still wasn't quite yet used to taking my infant around town alone. I was just trying to make it through the errand when I was confronted by a stranger about why my infant didn't have socks on. My baby didn't have socks on because it wasn't cold outside (we live in the southern U.S.), and she also never kept socks on, so it wasn't worth trying anymore. She was snuggled up in her car seat with a long sleeve comfy outfit on and blankets nearby, just in case she did get cold, but of course, this lady wasn't satisfied without my child wearing socks. She proceeded to lecture me about how infants *always* must wear socks.

I'm standing there, just trying to survive this outing, leaking breast milk, still sore, and she's talking to me about tiny socks and making me feel like a bad mom. (I'm sure my raging postpartum hormones did not help either.) I remember ranting to my husband afterward and I'll never forget what he said to me. "You know, you don't have to listen to her or take her advice, right? You can just choose to release it." Of course, I *knew* that somewhere deep down, but it was such a relief to hear someone say it out loud. From that moment in early motherhood onto the present day, I've tried to remember the freedom I have in parenthood to choose the advice I want to heed.

When someone gives you unsolicited advice, they are trying to get you to adopt and implement the decisions they made in their own parenting to your life. Without knowing you, your values, or your current circumstances, they think they know best.

Some parenting advice from friends, family, peers, and the internet is absolutely helpful. We are meant to collaborate with others so we can learn from others' experiences and acquire new skills. There will always be people who think their way is the right way and who will hand out unsolicited advice. We can't control that. However, we have control over how we react, where we draw the line, and what we decide to do with their advice. Keeping a positive mindset, especially with the use of positive affirmations, is crucial in helping you discern how to navigate this uncomfortable scenario.

"MY NEEDS OR MY CHILD'S NEEDS MAY DIFFER FROM SOMEONE ELSE'S, AND THAT'S OKAY."

Every child and every parent are different. Our differences are what make us unique. (Life would be extremely boring if we were all the same anyway.) What your child needs might not be what someone else's child needs. Also, if you have multiple children, each of them will have differing needs. Your child needing certain things, like occupational therapy, for example, doesn't mean you're failing. It simply means your child needs different resources than someone else.

Think of a time when you felt shamed or judged by someone for your parenting decisions. Write that person a brief statement or letter (without actually sending it) so you can release any baggage you may harbor about the situation.

Affirmations for

When You Miss Your Pre-Baby Self

"I'M STILL ME, EVEN THOUGH I HAD A BABY."

The all-consuming nature of parenthood makes it difficult to remember what life was like before it. Sometimes, this leaves us to romanticize our pre-baby lives. When we're standing in a valley, it's easier to dream and fantasize about the mountaintops. This makes us begin to miss times in our life and versions of ourselves that may not have been all that glamorous and happy, but when we're covered in spit-up and self-deprived, we may romanticize those pre-baby seasons.

The best way you can turn things around when you're missing your pre-baby self is to find ways to connect to your inner self outside of parenthood-related aspects. Underneath all the caregiving tasks and child-rearing, you're still you, and you deserve to stay connected to who you are at your core. In fact, your children will be better because of it.

"I WILL EXTEND MYSELF GRACE."

Extend the grace to yourself that you so freely give to your child. Be kind and gentle to yourself. Have patience with yourself as you learn and grow. You show this to everyone around you; you deserve to extend it to yourself as well while you navigate this new journey.

Affirmations for

Successful Co-Parenting

"WE SUPPORT EACH OTHER."

Parenting together works best when there's a deep sense of unity. Supporting one another in the process of parenthood is vital. Cultivating an environment of respect and teamwork will set an amazing example for your children. Sometimes, when disagreements occur, it can feel like the very person who is supposed to be our teammate is our enemy.

Your relationship will experience changes as a result of your baby joining your family if your co-parent is also your romantic partner. You will both make sacrifices, experience shorter tempers, and deal with bumps in the road as you learn and grow together. Unity and patience are so important as you handle these changes and situations, and your relationship will ultimately deepen and strengthen as a result.

"WE ARE A TEAM."

Whether you and your partner are in a relationship or not, learning effective co-parenting skills is crucial. Having a healthy co-parenting relationship is vital for your child's ultimate well-being. You have a shared goal: prioritizing your child's needs and happiness and keeping their best interest at heart. You both love your baby beyond belief. Because of this shared interest, you are a team. You both want to provide the absolute best for your children. It may be tricky sometimes to accomplish this since you're two different people, but at the end of the day, you are a team.

Affirmations for

When You Feel Worried

"MY BABY, MYSELF, AND MY FAMILY ARE SAFE."

It is common for new parents to feel frequent worry or anxiety regarding their baby's health and safety. The best thing you can do in your worried moments or while you're having anxious thoughts is to ground yourself. Staying grounded means focusing on the present moment without getting caught up in ever-changing emotions or intrusive thoughts.

Use your five senses to keep yourself grounded and connect to the moment when you're feeling anxious. The

54321 grounding exercise is very helpful in moments like these.

5: Take notice of five things you see immediately near you.

4: Recognize four things around you that you can touch.

3: Take notice of three things that you can hear.

2: Two things you can smell.

1: One thing you can taste.

54321 Exercise Practice

Next time you need to ground yourself when you're dealing with intrusive thoughts, try this exercise below to see if it helps you connect to the present moment. Over time, it may become second nature for you to do it internally.

Five things you can immediately see:

_____

Four things you can touch:

_____

Three things you can hear:

_____

Two things you can smell:

_____

One thing you can taste:

_____

"I'M IN CONTROL OF THE ENVIRONMENT OF MY HOME."

You obviously can't control everything that happens to everyone, but you can set the tone for the emotional environment of your home. It's up to the parents to control the emotional temperature of the family. It's not going to be perfect every day but it all just comes down to intentionality and baby steps.

Affirmations for
When You're Trying to Do It All

———

Parents wear many hats. The job is never-ending. It's a huge responsibility, and sometimes that can feel very daunting. We're highly motivated by our intense love for our children. We want to give them the best, provide for them, and help them however we can. However, the fact is that we simply cannot do it all.

You will run yourself into the ground trying to accomplish the impossible. Your baby needs you to be present with them for them to feel secure and grounded, but it's not possible to be present when you're juggling a million things. The following affirmations will encourage you to release unrealistic expectations and move forward with a bit more peace.

"MY SELF-WORTH AND VALUE AS A PARENT ARE NOT DEFINED BY HOW MUCH I ACCOMPLISH."

So often, we find ourselves attributing our worth to how much we're able to accomplish when, in reality, how much or how little you get done around the house has nothing to do with your character and your self-worth. Performing household tasks does not carry any moral significance. If you don't get the laundry done, that doesn't make you lazy. If the dirty dishes are still sitting in the sink, it doesn't mean you're failing. It simply means you're tired, overwhelmed, prioritizing family time, or you straight-up just don't feel like doing it.

Sometimes there are just way too many chores to get done, especially for only one person. This is where delegating comes in (which we'll talk about in the next affirmation.) Make sure your to-do list (whether it's a family list or a list for yourself) is realistic. Sometimes, I'll put the silliest, smallest things on my list, just to be able to cross them off. Seeing an item crossed off the to-do list is so gratifying! Even if your to-do list simply consists of "feed the baby, snuggle the baby, take a shower," it's just as satisfying to cross off. Think of your three major to-do's each morning, no matter how small or easy.

"IT'S OKAY TO ASK FOR HELP."

Let's just go ahead and get this out of the way: Asking for help doesn't make you a failure. Too often in our society, asking for help is synonymous with inadequacy and even failure. There's such an unfair stigma involved. It's assumed that, if you ask for help, that must mean you are incapable of accomplishing anything on your own. However, the truth is we all need a village. We're not meant to do this alone. Parenthood is a unique and challenging journey. It's also very rewarding. But it's certainly not meant to be navigated in solitude.

Your mental health is of the utmost importance. If your mental health is in a negative place, it will impact your children no matter how hard you try to hide it. Daily mental health routines and intentionality are vital for overall success. By watching you implement and carry out mental health routines for yourself, your children will internalize this and be better for it. It will teach them how to keep themselves mentally healthy as well.

Delegating helps the household to run smoothly. A practical way to delegate tasks and make sure you and your partner are both on the same page is to make an ongoing to-do list on a dry-erase board or piece of paper in a central location of the house. That way, you and your partner are both constantly aware of what needs to be accomplished and you two can both participate in tackling the workload.

There's that famous saying, "It takes a village to raise a child." The importance of having a village must not be underestimated. These days, a village doesn't have to be a physical village (although, it certainly helps.) Your village can consist of those in your online communities.

List the people in your village and reflect on how they contribute to your parenthood journey.

_____

_____

_____

"I CAN BE FLEXIBLE."

Flexibility is key in parenthood. Whether it's adjusting your baby's schedule on a whim or changing them into a backup outfit because of a blowout during an outing, the ability to be flexible is necessary. You'll be much happier the more flexible you're able to be. Being flexible mentally and emotionally is just as important as physical flexibility.

Sacrificing your own needs for the needs of another can be a really big adjustment in the early days of parenting, and no one really talks about this. Parents are typically expected to just immediately and easily acclimate, but the truth is, it turns your life upside down. Of course, when your life is turned upside down, it's going to take time to adjust.

Affirmations to
Empower You as a Parent

─────────
• ● •

"MY BABY LOVES ME NO MATTER WHAT TODAY MIGHT LOOK LIKE."

The innate love that you and your children have for one another overpowers any bad day. In early parenthood, you may feel like you're losing your mind. Your baby looks to you for support, comfort, love, and care. A bad or off day won't change that. Parental love plays an impactful role in developing a secure attachment between parent and child. The safer and more secure a child feels, the more success they will ultimately experience.

We all make parenting mistakes and do or say things we wish we didn't. However, it's a relief to know that the perfect parent does not exist. Perfection is just simply unachievable. So, take a load off. Let go of the unrealistic standards of perfection you've set upon yourself and lean into the unconditional acceptance and love that you and your child share.

"MY CHILD WAS MADE FOR ME. I'M THE BEST PARENT FOR THEM."

This one explains itself. Your child needs YOU. Not Suzy Q down the street with the perfect hair, unnaturally cemented smile, and freakishly-obedient children. Not Bob at the next cubicle over in the office. Your children need YOU just as you are. Believe it or not, no one is perfect, no matter what they may project or what it looks like on the outside. Everyone has their own struggles.

There's no one better for your children than you. Nature designed us to have innate bonds, strong connections, and automatic intuition to assist us in parenting. Lean into that. Trust yourself. You know more than you realize you do.

"I'M NOT MEANT TO KNOW EVERYTHING."

Can I give you a piece of advice really quickly? You're not supposed to know everything. It's impossible. Everyone has to learn somehow, someway. You don't know what you don't know until you learn it. You will learn as you go, and you may even surprise yourself with the innate knowledge and instinct you already have. The main way we gain knowledge throughout life is through experiences. With experiences, come inevitable mistakes. Release the unrealistic expectations you've placed on yourself.

Not only is it impossible to know everything right away, but we also can't be an expert in everything. Some areas of parenthood will be a strength of yours, while others will be not your strongest suit. And that's okay! You are learning something new every single day because parenthood is a process; there's no ultimate destination. You will never reach a time or place in which you feel you've satisfied every area of your parental role to perfection.

A practical way to work on releasing the self-induced unrealistic expectations: Every day, list one to three new things you learned that day either about parenting or your individual child. This is a tangible way to prove to yourself that you are acquiring new knowledge every single day, and this knowledge equips you as a parent even more.

"WHAT I DO NOT YET KNOW, I WILL LEARN IN TIME."

As we discussed earlier, parenthood is a process of refinement. We are constantly learning and growing. One of the most impactful mental health hacks I've learned is the power of "yet." "Yet" is one of the most influential words in my parenting vocabulary. Any time I can't do something, I will add "yet" to the statement, as I know I will eventually conquer it in time. You can flip any negative into a positive with "yet."

"I can't handle these tantrums...yet."
"I can't make it through the day without multiple naps...yet."
"I can't seem to keep up with parenting and household tasks at the same time...yet."

"Yet" gives you immediate space and grace to be patient in your parenthood learning process.

"I AM THE CHILDHOOD MAGIC MAKER."

Sometimes, it can be overwhelming to feel responsible for the cultivation of an ideal childhood for your kid. My encouragement to you is this: You are the perfect person for the job. You are the comforting nurturer, kisser of boo-boos, and maker of magic. Sure, it's a big responsibility, but it's also a great joy with the right perspective. It doesn't have to be perfect to be meaningful, special, and important to them. You get to create lasting traditions that are unique to your family, and even if your child is an infant, it's not too early to start!

Write down five things that you're proud of regarding your parenting.

What did you need most as a child that you didn't receive, and you can now work to give to your own child?

_____

_____

_____

Affirmations for

When It's Hard To Pack Up A Drawer

One of the hardest parts of parenthood is the swift passing of time. Everyone says how fast the little years fly by, but it's hard to fully grasp how that feels until you're experiencing it. Watching your baby change overnight throughout the first year and move from phase to phase can almost give a person emotional whiplash.

"I WILL FULLY EMBRACE TODAY."

When you get overwhelmed about time passing too quickly or your baby changing overnight, it's important to stay in the current moment. Smell their hair, take in all of their cute little features, hold their tiny hand, and simply *be.* Every moment you're given with your child is a gift, even the messiest of moments. Sometimes the best thing you can do for your bond is just spend time together.

Tomorrow, your child will be another day older. Tomorrow, their clothes will fit a little bit tighter. But today? Today, they're staying just as they are. Embrace today as it is.

"I WILL RESPECT AND COMPLETELY PROCESS MY EMOTIONS."

There is a level of grief and mourning involved in watching your child grow. You're mourning that version of them that you will not get to experience again in this life. However, on the other hand, it's so fun to watch them turn into who they're meant to be. We get a front-row seat to watching our children flourish in all of their individuality, and it's truly an honor.

Grief is actually quite a frequent aspect of parenthood that no one really talks about. I find myself constantly grieving as my children move from phase to phase. The excitement of new stages helps to put an uplifting spin on the grief, but there is such a heaviness that comes with the mere passing of time.

I'm the mom who cries as I pack up the contents of my child's dresser drawers and place them into storage tubs. (I'm usually not a crier so this is a major way parenthood has changed and affected me.) As I pack away the little articles of clothing, the tiny socks, and sentimental outfits, I also pack away that version of my child.

It's almost ceremonial. I always have to pack up the drawers by myself so I can process my emotions fully and privately, as I'm not personally able to fully process my emotions when others are watching. You owe it to yourself to take the space required for you to fully work through and *feel* your emotions. That way, you can move to the next stage carrying minimal emotional baggage from the stage before. Reciting affirmations during this time would serve as a comforting reminder to stay in the moment and create some helpful perspective to navigate the heavier moments.

"THE BEST IS YET TO COME. THIS IS JUST THE BEGINNING."

As a phase ends, it's a comfort to know that it's simultaneously the beginning of a new one. At the end of most stages of parenthood, there's usually a brand-new beginning that comes along with it. An ending with a simultaneous beginning...Another parenthood contradiction.

There is so much left for you to experience with your child as you walk through life with them. There are so many versions of them in the years ahead that you get to meet and embrace. This is the beautiful beginning of an incredible journey you get to be on together. While these words may not take away your grief and sadness, hopefully, it provides an optimistic perspective for your heavy heart.

"OUR FUTURE IS BRIGHT AND BEAUTIFUL."

Repeating this affirmation to yourself is a great reminder while you're in the early parenting trenches that there is so much joy ahead, no matter what has happened in the past. Your past does not ultimately determine your future. No matter who you used to be, what mistakes you've made, or what lies ahead, there is so much beauty to behold. You hold the power in determining what your future looks like, both in parenting and life in general.

Your actions are the only thing you can control, not your circumstances. Consider your values when reacting and responding to your circumstances. Your future is sure to be bright if your ambitions align with your values. Instead of getting wrapped up in any feelings of failure from your past, think about the lessons you've learned from any past mistakes, and how you can take these lessons with you into the future.

Affirmations to
Reaffirm Your Individuality

"IT'S OKAY FOR ME TO HAVE HOBBIES AND DESIRES OUTSIDE OF PARENTING."

Not only is it okay for you to have desires outside of parenthood, but it's actually healthy and encouraged! Your passions fuel your energy, and this carries over into other areas of your life. The dichotomy of personhood versus parenthood is an interesting one to experience. Parenthood is a refinement process. You're constantly growing and learning and adjusting. Parenthood also works as a mirror of sorts. You end up discovering new qualities about yourself that you may have never otherwise noticed or uncovered. It's so important to stay connected to who you are at your core while you're adjusting to parenthood.

People often talk about "finding yourself" and how important it is, but rarely does anyone talk about what this means or what it looks like practically. You hear stories time and time again of parents who completely give themselves up (or even their marriage/relationship up) during the years of active child rearing. Then, once their children grow up and move out, the parents have no idea who they are individually or as a couple. Due to this, many divorces occur after empty-nester status is achieved.

Stay connected to your true self. It's inspiring for children to watch their parents be in tune with who they are. It encourages individuality within themselves.

I grew up thinking my parents weren't human. They seemed so perfect as if they had no issues at all. Once I became an adult and we were able to have more of a friendship-type relationship, I realized they are very much human and imperfect. They feel raw, real emotions and have vulnerable moments, just like me.

Due to their desire to show a polished image, I was never able to see their vulnerability while growing up. This led to many feelings of inadequacy within me. I thought that, since my parents were perfect and I wasn't, something was wrong with me.

I never was able to see their true selves until later in life. Making these realizations about my parents changed my relationship with them and the way I view them and myself for the better. We were able to develop a much closer relationship, and I was able to feel higher self-worth myself.

My children know that I'm human. They know who I am and the characteristics that are connected to my true self. Watching me connect to my personhood encourages them to connect to theirs. As they see my husband and I's interests and strengths, they're able to learn that people are different. We all like different things, and not only is that okay, but it's so fun!

Don't lose sight of your true self in the baby years. Try not to make parenthood your entire personality. I know it's hard not to, simply due to the all-consuming nature of this season of life, but you deserve to continue being your own person outside of parenthood. Once your children grow up a bit more and need you less, you'll want to have your sense of self. They won't need you this much forever.

You still matter. You as a person, not just you as a parent.

Explain what makes you unique.

_____

_____

_____

What's your favorite quality about yourself?

_____

_____

_____

"I AM A BADASS."

Everyone has an inner badass. Whether you feel like it or not, you've got power, passion, and intensity within you that will help you through this new adventure of parenting. Harness it, lean into it, and fan that flame until it ignites an internal fire.

Finding Your Inner Voice

What narrative are you building about yourself throughout each day? Practice positive self-talk with the following fill-in-the-blank exercise.

I am a _____ parent.

No one can _____ like me!

I'm amazing at _____.

What makes me a badass parent is

_____.

Implementing Affirmations in Your Life

F or you to see and reap the benefits of regular affirmations, you must implement them into your daily life. The best way to do this is whatever way works best for YOU. There is no correct way to go about it.

Write them on your mirror. Put sticky notes all over the house. Make phone alarms or digital calendar events set to go off at times you need to read a certain affirmation. Say them quickly in your head or take the time to say them out loud to yourself in the mirror. Whatever your strategy or routine looks like, make sure it's realistic, easily achievable, and works best for you in your current season of life. Your routines may change as your circumstances change, and that's okay. Don't be hesitant to make adjustments if something's not working.

Each person's affirmation routine is unique. What you may benefit from in your affirmation routine, someone else may not need, and vice versa. That's why affirmations are so special; they can be personalized to your needs so that you can get what you need to get out of them. You can change any of these affirmations to best cater to you and what you personally need to empower yourself regularly.

Affirmations are a mental health game-changer. By utilizing affirmations in your daily routine, you will build your confidence and bravery, becoming the ultimate badass parent. Over time, the more you declare positivity over yourself, the more you'll believe it.

After all, you *can* do this.